BIG PICTURE 📷 SPORTS

Meet the CLEVELAND BROWNS

By
ZACK BURGESS

NORWOOD HOUSE PRESS

CHICAGO, ILLINOIS

Norwood House [logo] Press

P.O. Box 316598 • Chicago, Illinois 60631
For more information about Norwood House Press please visit our website at
www.norwoodhousepress.com or call 866-565-2900.

Photo Credits:
All photos courtesy of Associated Press, except for the following: Bowman Gum Co. (6),
Black Book Archives (7, 15, 22), Exhibit Supply Co. (10 top), Philadelphia Chewing Gum Co. (10 bottom),
Topps, Inc. (11 top & middle, 18, 23), NFL Pro Line (11 bottom).

Cover Photo: Eric Lars Bakke/Associated Press

The football memorabilia photographed for this book is part of the authors' collection. The collectibles used
for artistic background purposes in this series were manufactured by many different card companies—
including Bowman, Donruss, Fleer, Leaf, O-Pee-Chee, Pacific, Panini America, Philadelphia Chewing Gum,
Pinnacle, Pro Line, Pro Set, Score, Topps, and Upper Deck—as well as several food brands, including
Crane's, Hostess, Kellogg's, McDonald's and Post.

Designer: Ron Jaffe
Series Editors: Mike Kennedy and Mark Stewart
Project Management: Black Book Partners, LLC.
Editorial Production: Lisa Walsh

Library of Congress Cataloging-in-Publication Data
Names: Burgess, Zack.
Title: Meet the Cleveland Browns / by Zack Burgess.
Description: Chicago, Illinois : Norwood House Press, [2016] | Series: Big
picture sports | Includes bibliographical references and index. |
Audience: Grade: K to Grade 3.
Identifiers: LCCN 2015026324| ISBN 9781599537269 (Library Edition : alk.
paper) | ISBN 9781603578295 (eBook)
Subjects: LCSH: Cleveland Browns (Football team :
1946-1995)--Miscellanea--Juvenile literature. | Cleveland Browns (Football
team : 1999-)--Miscellanea--Juvenile literature.
Classification: LCC GV956.C6 B87 2016b | DDC 796.332/640977132--dc23
LC record available at http://lccn.loc.gov/2015026324

288N—072016
Manufactured in the United States of America in North Mankato, Minnesota

CONTENTS

Words in **bold type** are defined on page 24.

The Browns always look to make a little history.

CALL ME A BROWN

The Cleveland Browns like to make history. They won titles in the 1940s, 1950s, and 1960s. They were the first team to give starring roles to African American players. And many of the Browns' original ideas are still used in the National Football League (NFL).

The Browns are named after their first owner and coach, Paul Brown. They joined the NFL in 1950. Quarterback **Otto Graham** led them to three NFL titles. In 1996, the team moved to Baltimore and was renamed the Ravens. Cleveland then got a new team called the Browns.

Paul Brown meets with players before practice.

Empty seats are hard to find at a Browns game.

Best Seat in the House

The Browns have played in the same location since their first season. Their current stadium was built in 1999. It replaced an older stadium. Large pieces of the first building were dropped into nearby Lake Erie. They now form a reef for marine life.

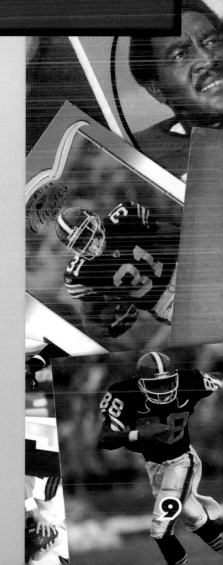

SHOE BOX

The trading cards on these pages show some of the best Browns ever.

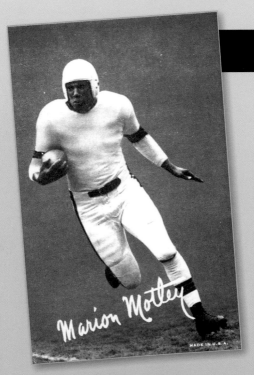

MARION MOTLEY

RUNNING BACK & LINEBACKER · 1946–1953

Marion was one of the most feared running backs ever. He helped make the Browns a championship team.

JIM BROWN

RUNNING BACK · 1957–1965

Jim was bigger, faster, and stronger than most of the defenders trying to tackle him. He was the NFL's top runner eight times.

LEROY KELLY

RUNNING BACK · 1964-1973

Leroy followed in Jim Brown's footsteps. He was an **All-Pro** each season from 1966 to 1968.

CLAY MATTHEWS

LINEBACKER · 1978-1993

Clay was always in the middle of the action. He made more tackles than anyone in team history.

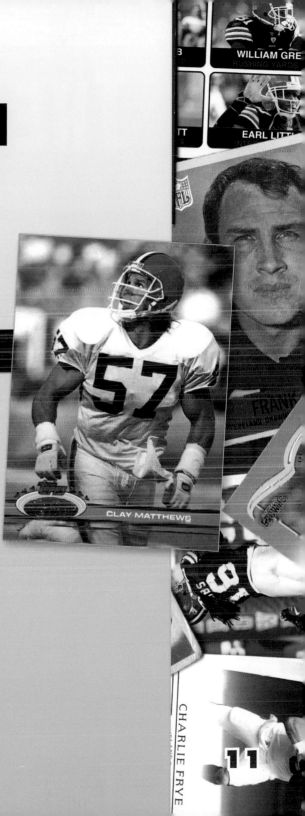

BERNIE KOSAR

QUARTERBACK · 1985-1993

Bernie was a favorite of the Cleveland fans. He led the team to within one win of the Super Bowl three times.

THE BIG PICTURE

Look at the two photos on page 13. Both appear to be the same. But they are not. There are three differences. Can you spot them?

Answers on page 23.

13

TRUE OR FALSE?

Joe Thomas was a star blocker. Two of these facts about him are **TRUE**. One is **FALSE**. Do you know which is which?

1. Joe was the third pick in the 2007 NFL **draft**.

2. Joe once played an entire game with one hand behind his back.

3. Joe played in the **Pro Bowl** in each of his first nine seasons.

Answer on page 23.

14

Joe Thomas is large and in charge.

Andrew Hawkins celebrates a score with the Dawg Pound.

Go Browns, Go!

Fans of the Browns are famous around the NFL. One section calls itself the "Dawg Pound." Fans in this area wear dog noses, dog masks, floppy ears, and bone-shaped hats. They can often be heard singing, "Here we go, Brownies, here we go. Woof! Woof!"

17

ON THE MAP

Here is a look at where five Browns were born, along with a fun fact about each.

 1 **BRIAN SIPE · SAN DIEGO, CALIFORNIA**
Brian was the NFL's Most Valuable Player in 1980.

 2 **DON COCKROFT · CHEYENNE, WYOMING**
Don was Cleveland's placekicker and punter for
13 seasons in a row.

 3 **OZZIE NEWSOME · MUSCLE SHOALS, ALABAMA**
Ozzie did not miss a game in 13 years with the Browns.

 4 **PHIL DAWSON · WEST PALM BEACH, FLORIDA**
Phil set a team record with six field goals in one game.

 5 **GERALD MCNEIL · FRANKFURT, GERMANY**
Gerald was nicknamed "Ice Cube" because he was small and slippery.

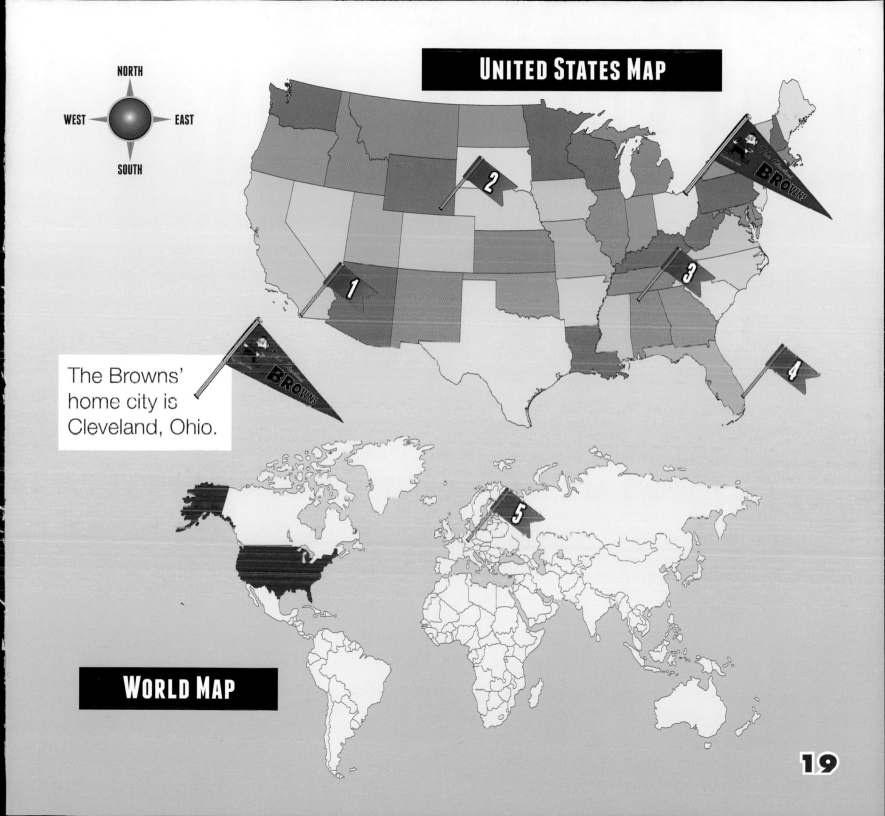

NORTH

WEST — EAST

SOUTH

1

2

3

4

5

The Browns' home city is Cleveland, Ohio.

WORLD MAP

Duke Johnson wears the Browns' home uniform.

Football teams wear different uniforms for home and away games. The main colors of the Browns are orange, brown, and white. They wear brown or orange jerseys at home.

The Browns'
helmet is very
simple. It is
orange with brown
and white stripes
down the middle.
This design has
changed little
since the team's
first season.

WE WON!

In 1948, the Browns went undefeated to win the **All-America Football Conference (AAFC)** championship. Receiver **Dante Lavelli** was one of the team's many stars. The Browns took four AAFC titles in all. After joining the NFL, they won four more titles.

RECORD BOOK

These Browns set team records.

TOUCHDOWN PASSES	RECORD
Season: Brian Sipe (1980)	30
Career: Otto Graham	174

TOUCHDOWN CATCHES	RECORD
Season: Braylon Edwards (2007)	16
Career: **Gary Collins**	70

POINTS	RECORD
Season: Jim Brown (1965)	126
Career: Lou Groza	1,608

GARY COLLINS

86

BROWNS

WIDE RECEIVER • A.F.C.

ANSWERS FOR THE BIG PICTURE
BROWNS disappeared from the left leg of the player on the far left, the football changed to a basketball, and #13 on the quarterback's left shoulder pad changed to #33.

ANSWER FOR TRUE AND FALSE
#2 is false. Joe never played a game with one hand behind his back.

FOOTBALL WORDS

INDEX

All-America Football Conference
A professional league that played from 1946 to 1949.

All-Pro
An honor given to the best NFL player at each position.

Draft
The meeting each spring when NFL teams select the top college players.

Pro Bowl
The NFL's annual all-star game.

Photos are on **BOLD** numbered pages.

ABOUT THE AUTHOR

Zack Burgess has been writing about sports for more than 20 years. He has lived all over the country and interviewed lots of All-Pro football players, including Brett Favre, Eddie George, Jerome Bettis, Shannon Sharpe, and Rich Gannon. Zack was the first African American beat writer to cover Major League Baseball when he worked for the *Kansas City Star*.

ABOUT THE BROWNS

Learn more at these websites:
www.clevelandbrowns.com   •   www.profootballhof.com
www.teamspiritextras.com/Overtime/html/browns.html